Learn How To Analyze People

An Essential Guide To Dark Secrets To Analyze And Influence Anyone Using Body Language, Human Psychology, Subliminal Persuasion And Nlp

By

DAVID GREEN

TABLE OF CONTENTS

INTRODUCTION

Thank you very much for purchasing this book.

Once you learn to read people and put it into practice, you will become good at it. Then, you can move on to the next step and start influencing the people around you.

Learn people's likes and dislikes and roll with them. Do you know someone who doesn't like big words or bad words? Don't do it around them. Do you know anyone who doesn't like violent things? Don't talk about that movie you saw in front of them.

Do you know anyone who likes fashion? Mention that you like their clothing. These are all subtle things that don't seem like much, but they make an important impression on the person you're interacting with.

If you do it enough, you will like them, regardless of other differences, and the more you make people like you, the more they will agree with your ideas.

Keep an open mind about people, they change, and so do you You should never form a universal opinion about someone. You can know how they are and you can support an opinion that you have formed (the right way), but never let it trap people.

If you know someone you have a bad opinion of, don't keep them there if they change.

Sure, you're allowed not to love some people, nobody likes everyone, but you don't have to put them in that box and keep them there.

The key to analyzing and reading people is to really know them and get to know them. The more you truly know someone, the better you will be able to influence them.

Chapter 1 History of Body Language

What is body language? Body language includes gestures, body posture, facial expressions, head, and eye movement.

Where Did Body Language Originate?

In fact, we can trace body language communication all the way back to our closest ancestors - the chimpanzees. Research scientists have proven chimpanzees not only communicate, but they also share similar emotions to humans. Dr. Jane Goodall teaches a Master class on the conversation and way of communication that she discovered takes place among the Chimpanzee community. Regardless of which species you study, the bottom line is that we all developed body language as a means of communication in the past. As we advanced and developed, we phased out certain actions and innovated new ones to help us better communicate and express our feelings and thoughts. Whether you're thinking about non-human body language communication such as how male gorillas stand up on two legs beating their chest as a sign of dominance or how primates bear teeth to communicate aggression or even how modern human beings send out emoji's instead of words to pass on a message these are all non-verbal signals that are meant to help us all express our current feelings and intentions.

While anyone can learn to read these signs, few have been trained to consciously do it or even use it proactively to their own benefit. Learning how to read body language, however, must begin with oneself. Unless you increase your awareness and understand what your own body is communicating, you don't stand a chance at effectively understanding what other bodies are telling you. So the first lesson is going to be, learning to decipher what your body is telling you, figuring out how you carry your own body and why you've been sending off the signals you usually send out.

Understanding What the Body Is Telling You

People are always communicating their true feelings through non-verbal cues, and so do you. Are you aware of what signals your body is sending as you interact with

others? If you think about it, body language can help you become what others call psychic or a mind reader because you'll be able to tell if someone is sincere, lying, pretending, or bothered by something at any given moment. There are many clues you can start looking out for as you interact with other people. I also encourage you to monitor yourself for the next seven days. Place a mirror where you eat, sleep, and lounge to see how you carry yourself. If it's at all possible, record yourself while working or in a meeting. Then take time to reflect on how you felt and what your body was saying during those moments. A few signals you can immediately start looking out for include:

• The body posture of another as well as your own.

• The smile on someone's face. Can you seek the corner of the eyes wrinkle and fold as the person smiles? Experts tell us that a real smile often creates a natural crinkle around the eyes.

• Is someone sneering while you speak? Are their eyes shifting all over the place? Do they seem constricted and "closed" in as they talk to you or open and relaxed?

These are just a few of the body signals you need to start noticing because they are all communicating something about that particular interaction. Why should this matter to you? Because the more you understand how others perceive you, the more you can control that perception. Another added benefit of this is that you'll be able to tell when someone is faking it with you. For example, my sister recently caught his boyfriend flirting with another woman. The guy apologized, and it seemed pretty heartfelt, but my sister could see in his eyes and from his body language that he wasn't sincere. She ended the relationship immediately after because she didn't

11

want to wait a year of being in a relationship with a man who was obviously not that serious about being faithful. Think of the heartache she just saved herself by calling it off earlier in the game before things got too messy. That is the power of having this skill set and using it effectively.

Human Reflex, Inevitable, or Not?

When an infant first sees a burning candle, the fascination of the fire usually causes them to reach out and touch it. I'm sure we've all had that same urge. But you and I both know our reflexes would kick in as soon as we attempted the foolish move of touching something hot like a burning candle flame. Yet the infant is most likely to end up getting burned because, for some reason, their brain doesn't register any action. Why is that?

Reflexes are there to protect us from danger. As we grow older, our reflexes get better, and we develop automatic responses that do not require the brain to create or direct any new action. Think of how fast you move your finger when you mistakenly touch a hot pan. What about when someone is about to slam the car door on your poor fingers? You'll most likely pull your hand away super-fast. That reaction is natural and very good because it's meant to protect you from losing your fingers or getting burned etc. These types of involuntary

12

responses, also known as reflexes, occur very quickly (most of them faster than the blink of an eye). But how do they work?

For your reflexes to work there must be excellent internal communication.

Your reflexes affect your body posture and sense of balance as well as coordination in more ways than you previously imagined. When your reflexes are working well, it's easy to maintain a strong body posture even without much conscious attention. From the moment you were born, learned to hold your neck up straight, sit, stand, and eventually walk, your reflexes have been working to stabilize your spine and, in turn, your posture. These, in turn, create rapid motor reactions involving the visual, proprioceptive, and vestibular systems. When any of these three systems are out of whack, you'll notice you have difficulty with coordination, controlling eye movements, controlling your posture, and you might even experience a lot of anxiety and fear.

As you can see, this can be an inhibiting factor if you want to learn how to analyze and read people's body language. When you have trouble controlling your body, it's going

to be tough reading that of another. There's also the common challenge that many of us unconsciously struggle with, whereby our bodies fall under the influence or control of primitive reflexes that no longer serve us. In such cases, individuals will find themselves overreacting, lacking the ability to control and automate the processing of simple movements and tasks. When that occurs, you'll notice the person appear overly nervous or "jerky" in his or her movement—for example, accidentally pouring a coffee in hand over a person instead of calmly stretching out your hand for a handshake. The bottom line is, you need to make sure your reflexes aren't working against you. If they are, that's the first change you need to make.

Breaking Down the Human Body

The body is complex, and there are many ways to approach understanding body language. I've simplified it to make sure you don't get bored with all the boring stuff.

Kinesics

This refers to body language or body movements in scientific terms. That includes gestures, head and hand movements, body posture, and whole-body movement. When we use our body, we can emphasize or reinforce what we are saying as well as better express a particular emotion or attitude. For example, suppose someone asked you how you're recent trip to Russia was, and you stood up from your chair, and then animatedly moved your body, shivering as if you were freezing. That person now has a much better sense of what you experienced. You could have easily said, "it was cold," and that would be that. However, by including full-body movement and emotion, the person got a much better sense of how cold the experience was for you. That is a simple example of how we use body movement to communicate. However, not all people match their words with their body movements. Being able to spot such discrepancies will help you know what someone is really thinking and feeling. Let's dive deeper into the various types of body movements. These include illustrators, emblems, regulators, adaptors, posture, and mirroring.

Illustrators - These are gestures that accompany words to illustrate a verbal message. The example of shivering in cold as you describe your Russian trip is an example of an illustrator. Another example would be making circular motion movements with your hands as you say the phrase "over and over again."

Emblems - These are gestures that serve the same function as a word. For example, Italians use a lot of emblems in their conversations, and in the American culture, we have hand movements that show you want to hitch a ride or that you're

15

summoning someone to call you. Depending on culture, emblems will vary, so make sure you use the right one to avoid miscommunication.

Regulators - These are gestures that give feedback to a person during a conversation. It helps you show interest and agreement or disagreement when engaging with someone else. Suppose you're having a conversation with a boss or family member. As they speak, you'll want to give feedback and let them know that you're paying attention by either nodding your head or making short sounds such as uh-huh. These are both examples of regulators.

Adaptors - These are non-verbal behaviors that a person usually does without conscious awareness. Most of the time, it will be a physical act that often reveals feelings of anxiety, nervousness, or even hostility. If you notice someone biting his or her fingernails (or if you bite your nails), that's an adaptive behavior indicating you're nervous. Someone might scratch, shake their legs, or adjust their glasses. Some girls are known to bite their hair or even twirl it around their fingers. These are all examples of adaptive behavior, trying to satisfy some psychological and physical needs.

Posture – We'll talk more about posture and the two main types of postures you need to become aware of (including their meaning), but for now, understand that posture is extremely important when analyzing people. Posture reflects emotions, attitudes, and even intentions. When you learn to read the cues someone's posture demonstrates, you can easily interpret hidden emotions, information, and personality without ever asking the other person what they want.

Mirroring - This is the ability to reflect what someone is showing you. Babies are professionals at imitation and mirroring what they see from their mom. If you observe two lovers sitting across a table having dinner, you'll also observe this mirroring effect.

Chapter 2 Reading Body Language like a Boss

From our outward appearances to our body developments, the things we don't state will in any case pass on volumes of information. It has been immediate that visual correspondence may account 60% to sixty five percent of all correspondences. Understanding visual correspondence is imperative, anyway it's furthermore fundamental to think to elective prompts like setting. In a few cases, you should investigate the flag as a gaggle rather than have practical experience in one activity.

Non-verbal communication is the implicit segment of correspondence. Our signals, outward appearances and stance, for instance. When we are prepared to "read" these signs, we can utilize it to further our potential benefit for instance. It will encourage you to know the whole message of what someone is making an endeavor to make reference to, and to fortify our consciousness of individuals' responses to what we are stating and do.

We can moreover utilize it to direct our visual correspondence, so we will in general appear to be a great deal of positive, sharing, and congenial.

Being able to communicate well is extremely important when wanting to succeed in the personal and professional world, but it isn't the words you say that scream. It is your body language that does the screaming. Your gestures, posture, eye contact, facial expressions, and tone of voice are your best communication tools. These have the ability to confuse, undermine, offend, build trust, draw others in, or put someone at ease.

There are many times when what someone says and what their body language says is totally different. Non-verbal communication could do five things:

• Substitute – It could be used in place of a verbal message.

• Accent – It could underline or accent your verbal message.

• Complement – It could complement or add to what you are saying verbally.

• Repeat – It could strengthen and repeat your verbal message.

• Contradict – It could go against what you are trying to say verbally to make your listener think that you are lying.

Some regular non-verbal communication signs.

The following are important hints to enable you to figure out how to read non-verbal communication and better understanding of the individuals you connect with.

Concentrate the Eyes

When human activity is towards someone, concentrate as to check whether the person in question looks or appearance away. Failure to make direct eye-to-eye connections will demonstrate boredom, impartiality, or maybe misleading – especially once someone appearance away and to the viewpoint. If an individual shows up down, on the contrary hand, it as a rule demonstrates anxiety or acquiescence. Additionally, check for extended students to check whether someone is reacting positively toward you. Understudies stretch as mental element exertion will in general increment, in this manner if someone is focused on someone or one thing they like, their students can precisely expand. Understudy widening will be hard to discover, anyway underneath the right conditions you should be prepared to spot it. An individual's squinting rate can even say a lot concerning what's going on inside. The squinting rate will increment once people are thinking a ton or are pushed. Now and again, swelled flickering rate shows lying – especially once over the span of contacting the face (especially the mouth and eyes). Looking at issue will guide a need for that thing. For instance, if someone looks at the entryway this could demonstrate they need to leave. Looking at an individual will demonstrate a need to address that person. When it includes eye conduct, it furthermore briefs that trying upwards and to the right communicated in language that demonstrates an untruth has been told, while attempting upwards and to one side shows the individual is telling the truth. The clarification for this can be that people search, and to the right ones exploitation, their creative mind to come up with a story, and appearance up and to one side once they are reviewing a genuine memory.

Look at the Face – Body Language Touching Mouth or Smiling

In spite of the fact that people are a ton certainly to deal with their outward appearance, regardless you'll have crucial nonverbal signals if you focus. Give explicit consideration to the mouth once making an endeavor to disentangle nonverbal conduct. A direct grin visual correspondence fascination procedure will be a hearty signal. Grinning is a critical nonverbal prompt to take a gander at for. There are various sorts of grins, together with genuine grins and affectation grins. A genuine grin draws in the whole face, while an imagining grin exclusively utilizes the mouth. A genuine grin proposes that the individual is upbeat and getting a charge out of the corporate of the people around the person in question. Covering the mouth or contacting the lips with the hands or fingers once talking is additionally a marker of lying.

Focus on nearness

Concentrate on letting someone stand or sit by you to check whether they read you positively. Standing or sitting in nearness to someone is perhaps one in all the best pointers of affinity. On the contrary hand, if someone backs up or moves away once you move in closer, this may be a proof that the alliance isn't common.

Check whether the other individual is reflecting you

Reflecting includes emulating the contrary individual's visual correspondence. Once interfacing with someone, check to analyze if the individual mirrors your conduct. For instance, in case you're sitting at a table with someone and lay an elbow on the table, hold up ten seconds to analyze if the contrary individual will be proportional. Another regular reflecting motion includes taking a taste of a beverage at a comparable time. If someone imitates your visual correspondence, this can be a terribly reasonable sign that the person is making an endeavor to decide an affinity with you. Endeavor dynamical your body stance and check whether the contrary individual changes theirs similarly.

Watch the head development

The speed at that an individual gestures their head once you are talking demonstrates

their understanding – or absence of. Slow hanging shows that the individual is entranced by what you're discourse correspondence and requirements you to keep talking. Fast hanging shows the individual has identified enough and necessities you to end talking or give that person a location to talk. Tilting the zenith sideways all through a communicated in language will be a proof of enthusiasm for what the contrary individual is discourse correspondence. Tilting the apex in reverse will be a proof of doubt or vulnerability. People also bring up with the face at others' significance they're captivated by proclivity with the individual.

Take a gander at the other individual's feet

A piece of the body any place people more often than not "release" fundamental nonverbal prompts is the feet. The clarification that individuals coincidentally impart nonverbal messages through their feet is therefore that occasionally they focus on their outward appearances and higher body situating which imperative pieces of information are unveiled by means of the feet.

Watch for hand signals

Like the feet, the hands release fundamental nonverbal 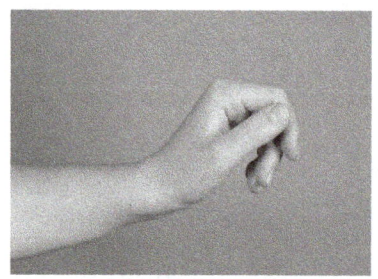 prompts once attempting a visual correspondence. This can be a critical tip once reading visual correspondence along these lines focus on the current next half. Watch visual correspondence turns in pockets once standing. Quest for explicit hand signals, similar to the contrary individual placing their hands in their pockets or hand on head. This may show something from apprehension to out and out trickiness. Oblivious educate demonstrated by hand motions can even say a lot. Once making hand signals, an individual can with reason inside the general course of the individual offer a partiality (this nonverbal prompts is indispensable to take a gander at for all through gatherings and once connecting in gatherings). Supporting the apex with the hand by laying an elbow on the table will demonstrate that the individual is tuning in and is keeping the zenith still to center. Supporting the zenith with every elbow on the table.

When an individual holds an item between the people in question and along these lines the individual they're collaborating with, this is a boundary that is intended to dam out of the contrary individual. For instance, if two people are talking and one individual holds a stack of paper in front of that person, this can be demonstration of check in nonverbal correspondence.

Inspect the situation of the arms

Think about an individual's arms as the door to the body and in this way oneself. If an individual folds their arms while interfacing with you, it's occasionally observed as a guarded, impediment signal. Crossed arms can even demonstrate nervousness, weakness, or a shut personality. Whenever crossed arms are throughout a genuine grin and generally speaking loosened up stance, at that point it will demonstrate all is guaranteed, loosened up edge. When someone puts their hands on their hips it's for the most part they need to apply strength and is utilized by men a great deal than women.

Body parts

Lower Body

The arms share a lot of information. The hands share a lot more, but legs give us the exclamation point and can tell us exactly what someone is thinking. The legs could tell you if a person is open and comfortable. They could also who dominance or where they want to go.

Legs Touching

When a person is standing, they will only be able to touch their bottom or thighs. This can be done seductively, or they could slap their legs as if they are saying "Let's go." It might also indicate irritation. This is when you have to pay attention to the context of the conversation. This is very important.

Pointing Feet

Look at the direction of a person's feet to see where their attention is. Their feet will always point toward what is on their mind or what they are concentrating on. Everyone has a lead foot and it all depends on their dominant hand. If a person is talking that we are interested in is talking, our lead foot will be pointing toward them. But, if they want to leave the situation, you will notice their foot pointing toward an exit or the way they want to go. If a person is sitting during the conversation, look at where their feet are pointing to see what they are truly interested in.

Smarty Pants

This is a position where someone tries to make they look bigger. They will usually be seated with their legs splayed open and leaning back. They might even spread their arms out and lock them behind their head. This is normally used by people who feel dominant, superior, or confident.

Shy Tangle

This is usually something that women do more than men. Anyone who begins to feel shy or timid will sometimes entangle their legs by crossing them under and over to try to block out bad emotions and to make them look smaller. There is another shy leg twirl that people will do when they are standing. The actual act of this movement is crossing one leg over the other and hooking that foot behind their knee as if they are trying to scratch an itch.

Upper Body

Upper body language can show signs of defensiveness since the arms could easily be used as a shield. Upper body language could involve the chest. Let's look at some upper body language.

Chapter 3 Non-Verbal Body Language

Nonverbal communication is the main aspect of which people base their first impressions on. Due to this fact, it is crucial that we build a good understanding of what our body language comes off as to other people. By doing this, we can better understand other people's body language; thus, helping us analyze them. We do this already in our day to day life simply because we are visual creatures. Our eyes perceive the world around us, and this is no different when perceiving people. Learning what to look for and how to decipher this type of communication involves fine-tuning a skill that each of us already possesses. You can almost quickly profile anybody just by assessing their nonverbal communication skills.

What Does Nonverbal Communication Mean?

Before we dive into the details of body language, what does nonverbal communication actually mean? This term defines the different ways that people can communicate without the use of words. This involves things that people do (or do not do) that send messages about what they think and feel. People typically are very careful when it comes to sharing information with other people. This type of physical, bodily communication can be either a conscious or unconscious action, meaning that we may not even know that we are sharing our thoughts, feelings or opinions in ways other than through our words.

Different Types Of nonverbal Communication

This is the first step in learning to analyze a person. I have made a list for you to simplify things, study this thoroughly as these are the types of cues you should look out for in yourself and others when it comes time for practice.

1. Facial Expressions

The first types of body language cue I will be teaching you

 about are facial expressions. The faces our parents made to make us laugh or the faces they made when

they were unhappy with us. As babies, we are attuned to the facial expressions of our caregivers as we are nonverbal creatures at this age. Into adulthood though, facial expressions are still a very trustworthy and sometimes not-so-subtle way of reading a person. The faces people make when sad, happy, angry or afraid are universal- they are innately human and do not vary among cultures or languages. Learning to control your own facial expressions will allow you to convey the message you want to deliver, whether you actually mean it or not. On the other hand, learning to analyze them on other people will allow you to get a more accurate read on how this person is feeling and what thoughts are going on in their mind.

2. Eye Contact

The next type of body language we will look at is visual

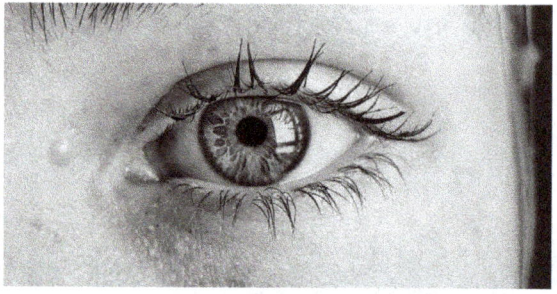

communication. The eyes are usually the place we look when we are having a face to face interaction

with someone. The eyes can tell so much about one's thoughts and feelings. The actions they take, such as how long they will hold our gaze if they will even make eye contact at all, or how often they are blinking can give us information about what is going on behind them. I will dive deeper into different eye movements and gazes and what they could mean.

3. Hand Gestures

Gestures are deliberate signals or movements that are done to convey a message. These can be used to replace verbal communication on purpose. Think of the signals you may use to communicate a message when you are in a very loud place or when you are trying to communicate to someone without letting the other people in earshot know what you are saying.

4. Space

Space is the next type of nonverbal communication we will discuss. This can vary greatly between societies, but in general, you can determine how someone feels in your presence and about what you are saying by how much space they leave between you and them. In some cultures, it is normal to stand very close to someone when you are speaking to them, and in others that would be considered very intrusive. The key here, however, is to know what the individual person's default amount of distance would be and use that as a guide. Many times, when you are immersed in an unfamiliar culture, you may think that someone is being 'rude' or too 'touchy' when simply they may just have a different cultural norm of space.

5. Touch

Another form of body language similar to space is touch. Touch varies greatly between societies and cultures but in any case, we as humans respond to touch. Sometimes touch will indicate that someone is empathizing with what you are saying, and they are breaking the space barrier between you in order to show you that they are supportive. Sometimes the person feels comfortable with you and they will use touch as a gesture to communicate a certain point in a story or explanation. On the flip side of this though, sometimes touch is used in a more negative context. Sometimes touch is used to demonstrate power or superiority. People will sometimes place their hand on your shoulder or on your head as a way of saying that they are above you and are in control of you. People may use touch in order to force something they wish by taking an object from your hand or physically moving you out of their way.

Touch is a form of nonverbal communication that can demonstrate either extreme closeness or extreme distance and disdain. The way that it is done will demonstrate very different messages. An example of this is at the beginning of a relationship, where the first instance of touch is a nonverbal way of sending a big message. To that point though, it can also work in reverse. On a date, if the other person keeps their distance by staying at arm's length and avoiding touch completely, this can tell you that they likely are not interested in pursuing anything further.

They may also use touch to show us that we have been bad by spanking us on the behind. A simple touch can contain an immense amount of information.

6. Vocal Dynamics

You may be thinking that vocal dynamics may fall under  verbal communication; however, there is a whole lot more to a message than just the words in it. The way that someone delivers a sentence is much more telling than the words it contains. For example, the inclusion of a pause or a drawn-out word and even complete silence can tell you about a person's internal state. If a person becomes suddenly silent, they may be offended by the topic of conversation or by something that was said. If the person avoids silence at all costs, they are likely a nervous or anxious person who is uncomfortable with a silent moment or two. The tone of voice and volume play a huge part in this as well. If you didn't understand a word that someone was saying but could read their verbal communication cues, you would be able to tell a lot about what they were trying to convey. Like facial expressions, this is another type of nonverbal communication that we learn when we are very young. We can tell the difference between a happy and an angry sentence even before we have a full vocabulary to use and understand the meaning of the sentence. The volume of a person's voice can also indicate traits of their personality or their current state. If they are speaking very quietly, they are probably shy or nervous, while a loud volume can mean that they are angry or excited. A great example of the tone of a person's voice demonstrating more than what their words are saying is sarcasm. When we are using sarcasm, the tone of our voice is exactly the opposite of what we are saying. If someone were to misunderstand our tone, they would become very confused as to what we meant. If we say, "I loved waiting in line for four hours", the tone we say it with indicates that we actually mean exactly the opposite.

7. Appearance

This type, however, is still important to note as it aids in forming a first impression of a person, especially from afar. The colors people choose to wear, the types of garments they choose and the level of perceived effort or time one has put into their outward appearance all play into our analysis of them. For instance, if you seem someone that is

dressed in all black, metal chains, spikes, dark make up and a Mohawk hairstyle, you may assume that they are unfriendly. However, if you speak to this person, you may find out that it may actually be the opposite. The way you shape your appearance and the way others choose to appear to play a huge role in what you think of them and how others will think of you.

8. Energetic Changes

The next type of nonverbal communication that we will examine is Energy or energetic changes that a person's body may give off. If you have ever felt that there was something causing you to feel uncomfortable or awkward in a situation or a room where nobody has spoken and where there are no signs of body language telling you there is something going on in other people's minds, this could be the type of energy we are talking about. There are places within our bodies that actually create electrical signals such as the heart and the neurons in our brains. While the concept of energy is a relatively novel one within the psychology field, it is no doubt they're in our bodies. There may be a type of nonverbal communication that we can pick up on from others' bodies that makes us feel certain ways in response. Some use the term 'vibe' to explain the things we feel but cannot see and have a difficult time explaining with words.

9. Bodily Changes

A type of nonverbal communication that is completely out of our control is the bodily changes that happen when we feel certain emotions. Some people may turn red in the face when they are embarrassed. Some may begin shaking when they are enraged, and some people's eyes widen, and their pupils dilate. When we have a sudden rush of fear or feel threatened, we have an automatic bodily response that is caused by the release of adrenaline. This happens automatically to all of us and dates back to our days as early humans and cavemen. When we were hunter-gatherers and had to live outdoors and hunt our own food, we were constantly threatened by the potential danger of predators, natural disasters or enemy tribes. Because of this, we needed to have a natural instinct to save ourselves. When we feel afraid, our body responds by causing our pupils to dilate, our bodies to stiffen, heart rate to increase and our breathing to change. All of these responses are to prepare us to face the issue causing us to be afraid.

Chapter 4 How to Fake Your Body Language

Faking body language is not easy because there is always something that is going to sell you out. It could be the eyes are not accompanying the smile, the hands are not accompanying the words, and the head is not following the hands and many more others. However, despite the entire sell out, body language faking can be learned so it means it is possible to fake your body language. You do not need to fake 100 percent of your body language because there will be a hitch, but you can always fake 70 percent of it. For you to fake your body language, you must first understand how to learn and interpret body language. It is like a basketball game, you cannot be good at basketball if you haven't learned about its rule, the risks involved, the importance of the game and the remedy if you are not achieving the expected results.

In body language faking, just like in the example above, you must know what your expectations are. Why are you faking it? You must know how good you are. This means you should try it on someone you know and ask them what they think. You must understand the body language you want to fake very well before attempting otherwise it will shame you.

Faking body language should be used for the common good rather than in a conspicuous way. When some people fake body language it boosts confidence in them and others. There are different ways you can fake your body language to suit your desires. Below are a few of the ways to do it;

Taking In a Deep Breath

When talking to someone whether you are giving a speech to the audience or you are listening to them, you should watch both the breathing rate and the other persons. The breathing rate of a person tells much about your emotions. Breathing of a person and his emotions are highly connected so you must be very careful with your rate of breathing if you want to fake it. When someone breaths deeply, it might show that he is afraid. A person holding his breath for some time than breathing deeply shows that the person is afraid. For example, a child who knows that after telling his mother that he licked sugar will be beaten, no matter how the mother asks him; he will simply breathe deeply without speaking.

He is sending a message to his mother that he is afraid that if he speaks, he will be beaten. So if you are afraid and you do not want to show the other person, you want to feel more superior, you want to prove that you are not afraid of doing anything or you are not afraid of the other person, make sure your breathing rate is balanced. You should not breathe in deeply once after he has asked a question, take time breathing normally, you can hold your breath a little bit then start breathing normally, someone won't recognize the fear you are experiencing.

Taking a deep breath may also signify anger. When someone is angry, he has no control over the thing or the one upsetting him. Just like fear, anger is emotional and like we said emotional feelings are connected to breathing. When you are so upset and so angry, watch your breathing rate if you do not want to show it. To fake your breathing rate, you can smile a bit and sip some water if there is any in the glass instead of breathing deeply. Maintain your eye contact and think of funny things in your past, use humor, like crack a funny joke when the person aiming to make you angry says an awful thing, you can also repeat a calming phrase within your head like 'take is fine, take it easy'. This will help calm you down and you will realize your breathing rate is normal.

Deep breath also shows excitement. This could be excitement from receiving after party. You are excited that it was a wonderful party, but if you happened to sneak out of the house and go to this wonderful party and you come back to find your parents waiting for you, you have to fake it because party on a school day is guaranteed with punishment. To fake it you should make sure you do not breathe deep in with a wide smile on your face. Not doing this will make your parents see your excitement and know what you were up to.

When someone is relieved, he is likely to take a deep breath. Thus taking a deep breath signifies relief. You may have been fighting with someone over a piece of land for a year, and then he comes to you and says he has let it go, you can have it. This is a relief. You will take a deep breath for that. You can always fake this so that he can see how tiring the case was to you.

When you breathe in deeply, it might also show shock, surprise which is always accompanied by a head sign, love attraction, hopelessness or sadness. If you have to fake all these, you must make sure your breathing stays normal no matter how much these feelings flood your mind. To make sure you want to fake all your emotional traumas or feelings without anyone knowing they are fake; it is also good that you identify your emotional triggers. This will help you be in charge of your emotions and each time any trigger is pressed, you will find yourself smiling about it and it will not affect you. This way you would have faked it beyond any doubt.

Controlling the movement of your eyebrows

The eyebrow movement will tell what you are thinking and the message you are trying to pass across. By lowering your eyebrows when speaking to someone it will send a variety of messages. When your eyebrows are lowered, it shows deception. You will be concealing something from the audience or the speaker. If you want to fake this even if you are hiding something, make sure your eyebrows are raised humbly. This will send a different message. Lowered eyebrows also show desire. The desire that the eyes cannot see or are afraid to view. For example- in a love relationship, when a partner asks for a kiss, you might find yourself lowering your eyebrows. This is sending a message that you have the desire to kiss but you can't say it, or the eyes can't help it. If you want to fake this so that the other person does not see that you have no desire, you can act surprised by raising your eyebrows with your eyes open wide or do exactly what is required. This will tell the person of your surprise or your desires in the kiss too.

A person lowering eyebrows may also be annoyed. Annoyance may be caused by a variety of things and he is afraid that if he raises his eyes he might cry or be tempted to say something bad. If you want to fake it so that nobody can know if you are annoyed, you can start breathing in and then out as you count, or focus on the main aim of the conversation and you will realize that your annoyance is subsiding and while doing all this, let ensure your eyebrows haven't changed their former position.

Raised eyebrows may signify attention requests or demands depending on the question posed before the raising.

Demanding for attention with raised eyebrows is seen rude sometimes especially if it is coming from a child to a parent or a younger person to an older on so you should be careful if you have this habit. Faking this raising of eyebrows when asking for attention, you may show attraction instead, when someone sees attraction in the eyes, he will give the attention you want. This attraction can be done by raising your eyebrows to expose your eyes.

Submission can also be symbolized by raised eyebrows. For example, a person asking you if you are going to lend him money and you raise tour eyebrows. This means you have submitted to his request and he will get the money. But if you do not want the person to see that you are forcing this submission, you can as well lower your eyebrows, he will be confused and won't tell if it is a yes or no or you can raise your eyebrows with the eyes looking up, this will tell the person that you are thinking about it.

Raising one eyebrow can also indicate cynicism especially when the other person is speaking inaccurately. The other person may feel offended if he saw you cynically raising your eyebrows thus to fake it, you can stay with your eyebrows normal but focus your mind on something else. When he is done talking you greet each other and leave like nothing ever happened. Most of the psychologists use this faking especially to the clients who are so depressed and are speaking things that do not make sense, the psychologists even go ahead and nod their heads while the clients are speaking then they can now paraphrase their words to get clarification otherwise raising one eyebrow to them will confuse them more and they will be annoyed that they are not getting the help they needed.

Pushing together your eyebrows and pulling up your forehead indicated relief. For example, you have been waiting for a whole day for some news from the interview you attended, then finally the results come and you have passed. This is a great relief and you will feel your nerves calming down. This way your eyebrows will be pushed together and forehead pulled up. To make sure that someone believes in this you as it is written. Anxiety can also be seen when the eyebrows are pushed together, and the forehead pulled up. You can fake anxiety especially when you want to get out of a boring meeting that you have by saying you have to see a doctor. The show of anxiety on your face can get you permission to step out.

Relaxing your face

A relaxed face is not a compressed face. A relaxed face can easily be seen by the facial muscles. The muscles are flexed, the eyebrows not clenched together, the forehead is not wrinkled or creased, the eyes are not tensed and the lips are full. All these describe a relaxed face. If anything from the above is opposite, this means you do not have a relaxed face and anyone can be able to tell what is bothering you. To fake a relaxed face, you have to understand the following facial meanings;

A relaxed face shows control of emotions. It tells you that you are in control of what is going on around you.

For example, you indulge in an argument at the office with your co-worker, the shouting is so high from your fellow worker that the other workers come in, just by the calmness on your face, and the other workers will see control of your emotions. They will know that you have the situation under control and it is not bothering you.

Chapter 5 How to Detect Deception

Everything considered, we should endeavor to find out for ourselves. There might be some tell-tale signs that you can look out for to tell whether somebody is cheating. Do you have the option to tell which one, expecting any, is a lie?

The ordinary individual hears some place in the scope of several misrepresentations for every day. Outcasts lie to each other on numerous occasions inside the underlying few minutes of social interactions, everything considered.

As demonstrated by scientific studies, the suitable reaction is: they are all substantial. So, on the off chance that we are being misdirected that much of the time, by what method may we make a better appearing with respect than of getting the prevaricators we partner with?

There are practices and tells that should make you wonder whether the individual you are overseeing is being straightforward. Here are a number of things to scan for to tell whether somebody is not truthful.

1. Qualifying language

People who are being clear at times prefer to exhort you that people, when all is said in done, aren't always veritable. How? By using articulations like, "In all genuineness" or "on the off chance that I'm as a result absolutely legitimate" or "In case I expected to swear on a store of Bibles - "

Be careful for these. Think of it as like that old saw "In case you have to solicit, you cannot endure its expense." Here, in case you have to underscore that you are confessing all, you likely could be lying.

2. Repeating the request

Maybe they are ensuring they heard you precisely. Or of course, maybe they are backing off for a time, or else endeavoring to empty what you have solicited and understand the sum you know. In case they are doing this, note it, and check it with a bit of the other on the summary.

3. Abnormality

It is essentially too much straightforward, and deluding, to rely upon inconsistency as a middle person for misleading.

All things considered, most legitimate people, when they are drawn closer to retell a story a couple of times, which means the records they tell will change.

4. Inconsequential superlatives

There are times when the words really, absolutely and literally are appropriate, yet they are the uncommon case to the standard. People who request peppering their talk with them may endeavor to bolster their dispute or trying to hide something from you.

5. Inappropriate emotions

You are scanning here for disarray: loathsome news, anyway a joking manner to the extent anybody knows inspiring news, anyway too much tempered excitement. The display of emotions can indicate that somebody is desperately trying to hide something from you particularly if the emotions are unwarranted. If you find that you are having a conversation with somebody and they cannot control their emotions, it might be prudent to assume that they are lying about something they are saying.

6. A hankering to shut everything down

They would incline toward not to talk, or they have to move the discourse along quickly to another subject. Is that since you are that debilitating a conversationalist or possibly they are on edge to move out of the zone of misleading into an increasingly secure space? Yet again, this is unquestionably not a protected tell, yet it is another piece of verification to consider as you measure the likelihood that you are being told something untruthful.

7. Winds in the word no

Vital tells could be when people "express no and look in another bearing," "express no and close their eyes," "express no in the wake of vacillating," "state no, stretched out over a huge part of time," or "express no in a tedious manner."

One way to trap them is to force them to express the word no to an inclined or open-completed request. "Did you record a sham cost report?" as opposed to "I'm intrigued about the precision of our cost reports. Do you have any information into that?"

8. Scorn

Disdain does not mean in a general sense that someone is lying, yet it implies that you should reconsider the talk. Since hatred is a blend of disturbance and great commonness, it is essentially hard to make partiality with someone who feels that way.

It is shown by one lip corner pulled up and in; it is the primary uneven enunciation. Additionally, inside seeing hatred, paying little mind to whether deception seeks after - and it does not, for the most part, seek after - look the other way, go the other course, reconsider the plan, express, "No, favor your heart. I'm not coming up for just a single additional nightcap.

Remember, these are generally potential bits of confirmation. No one of them shows without a doubt that somebody is lying, and it is also possible to get false positives. Look, tune in, test, represent some hard request, get away from that genuinely pleasing strategy for knowing, walk around intrigue mode, present more requests, have a little pride, and treat the individual you are talking with similarity. Solidify all that, and you will have a very savvy thought whether you are being lied to or not.

9. Fail to recall nuances subsequent to retelling

This is exceptional: it is where the individual talking does exclude new nuances that discredit one, yet what's more cannot survey what the individual as of late said.

One way to ascertain this is to ask them to relate to the story in turn around. It is only harder to keep nuances straight on the off chance that you are mentioning that they relate a made up story in a startling solicitation in contrast with they learned it.

10. Suspicious verbalizations

There are a couple of tells that can propose nonappearance of veracity: blushing, squinting, flared nostrils, fake smiles. Notice them, recall them, center. Regardless, don't scrutinize a great deal into them

Since while they may be signs, there is only a great deal of room for false positives to go by verbalizations alone. It is very inconvenient despite for readied, experienced insightful pros to pick a liar dependent on outward appearances.

You find the opportunity to manage a specific morning and as you prepare to get involved, an accomplice passes by your work territory, invites you and requests what you think from her new dress.

You quickly uncover to her how lovely it looks on her, paying little heed to whether you think it makes her look slob. You just deceived your partner, yet she walks around to her work territory with a smile everywhere.

Lying is essentially second to human intuition. Most by far of us tell a few blameless embellishments reliably. We furthermore get deceived a similar measure. One examination shows that the Average American local deceptions on different occasions every week. We lie much more than we might think and this might affect our overall relations with other people and even the manner in which we communicate. Lying is almost an essential part of all of us.

Men are said to delude their assistants, administrators, and work relate an ordinary on different occasions every day. The lying happens for different reasons. Most by far who falsehood do all things considered to guarantee themselves or the other individual by one way or another or another, either from being settled on a choice, from troublesome emotions or from disgrace.

A significant part of the time where we get misdirected, the misrepresentations are ordinarily harmless. Once in a while, it is amazingly preferable to be deluded over to be confessed all. For instance, when you hoodwinked your accomplice over that she looks incredible in her new dress; it improved her vibe than if you had uncovered to her what you truly think.

Regardless, lies can every so often have tremendous impacts.

Lies about huge issues can incite basic results like finding ended from a profession, broken associations, or even jail time. Finding that someone misdirected you can break down all the trust you have in them and perpetually change how you relate with each other.

If people lie so often, by what method may you avoid being compelled to hold up under a misrepresentation?

Luckily, there are some powerful advances that you can take to end up being better at sniffing out when someone is empowering you a stack of it. Consider the following additional advice to understand when somebody is lying to you:

Pose the Same Inquiry Multiple Times

In the event that you think somebody is sustaining you a heap of it, take a stab at asking them a particular inquiry around three unique occasions. Scrutinize the expression during the inquiry contrastingly each time. Watch out how they answer the inquiry. Does their answer change dependent on how you stated the inquiry, or do they continue giving a similar answer again and again?

On the off chance that somebody continues giving a similar answer paying little mind to how you outline your inquiry, there is a high possibility that they are giving you a practiced answer.

Somebody who is coming clean will give an answer that sounds less scripted. Somebody who has encountered something will have different methods for portraying the experience. Be that as it may, if the experience is made up, they will need to adhere to a content to abstain from making mistakes.

Look to See If They Are Stressed

The weight response in the psyche accordingly triggers some physiological weight markers, for instance, squirming, foot tapping, yawning, getting to be flushed, and sweating, and so on.

A portion of the time, the individual may contact their nose attempting to calm down their brain. In case you see any of these signs when presenting the request, there is a believability that the individual may lie.

The best way to deal with chooses if an individual is lying by watching weight markers is to consider these pointers against a standard.

If the individual does not normally show any of the above practices until you start examining them with respect to a particular issue, this implies they may lie.

Go with Your Instincts

A few people are extremely gifted at lying, and will effortlessly do as such without giving any tells. Now and again, you will run over such a liar. Attempt as you may, you won't recognize any giveaways.

In any case, you may feel that the individual is lying, regardless of whether you cannot point to any single thing as the explanation for the inclination.

Commonly, this hunch depends on something genuine. Try not to disregard it.

Lying is a piece of human instinct, and there is no single, all-inclusive technique that you can use to distinguish when somebody is deceiving you. A portion of the techniques referenced above will take a shot at certain liars however not on others.

Likewise, the techniques and pointers referenced above do not carefully imply that the individual is lying. Rather, they demonstrate that there is a probability that the individual may lie.

The most ideal approach to measure in the event that somebody is lying is to utilize a blend of these techniques.

Chapter 6 Body Language Secrets

When you try to know more about your goal and how they view the world, body language is going to be so crucial. Too many times we get caught in the words that someone else tells us and we won't concentrate on the other indications they also give us. There is so much that can be disclosed by these body language clues, and it makes a large difference in how effective you are in understanding and working with your goals.

Body language will refer to some of the nonverbal signals we use to interact with others. These nonverbal signals will take up much of the interaction we communicate every day. From the movement of our body to our facial expressions and everything in between, things we don't say can still share a ton of information during the process. Indeed, 60 to 65% of our interaction could be accounted for by body language and other nonverbal communications. So how do we learn to read this language to our own advantage? Let's begin by learning more about the various indications of body language, and how we can read this for our benefit. First of all, we have the facial expressions.

Think of a time, by the expression on your face, about how much data someone can convey. A smile is a nice way to show happiness or consent. A frown can imply the other way around. In some instances, facial expressions can show our real emotions about a scenario. While an individual may say he's okay, he looks like he's talking when he says this might talk otherwise. There are many feelings on our facial expressions, including:

1. Contempt

2. Desire

3. Excitement

4. Confusion

5. Fear

The expression that appears on the person's face helps us to determine if we trust and think anything the person says. In reality, one research discovered that the most credible of all facial expressions will be a small eyebrow raise and a slight smile. This is an expression that in many instances shows us to trust and friendliness.

The other type of body language cue will have to be the mouth. Mouth expressions and motions can be another vital component of body language reading. For instance, if you notice someone else chewing on his bottom lip, it may show that there are feelings of insecurity, fear, and worry. The individual can cover his mouth to be polite when he coughs, but sometimes the other person's disapproval. And smiling will be one of the best signals of corporeal language, but the smile and what it says about a person can be evaluated differently. Some of the stuff you can care about when reading someone else's mouth movements include:

Pursed lips: If you see your goal tightened up, it's a sign of distrust, disagreement, and disgust.

Lip biting: This is when you bite your lower lip, usually when you are stressed, anxious, or distressed.

Mouth cover: Any moment someone wishes to conceal one of their emotional responses, they can cover their mouths in order to assist.

Turned up or down: Even a slight shift in your mouth can be a subtle indication of how you feel right now. When your mouth turns up, it's a sign that you are hopeful or glad. It could be a grimace, disagreement, and even sorrow when the mouth turns down.

Another area to observe as body language cue is gestures.

Gestures can be a very evident, direct sign of body language to be careful about. Waiving, pointing and fingering can be common and easy to understand gestures. Some may even be cultural. Some of the most popular gestures and the significances that come with them include:

A clung fist: In most cases, this will show anger, but sometimes it can also imply solidarity.

Up or down thumbs: This is used as a sign of approval and disapproval.

The "all correct" gesture: This one will assist others to say you're fine in the United States. But it is seen in some other cultures as a vulgar gesture.

The next thing we have to do is look at the arms and legs of the individual you talk to. These can be useful if a lot of information is to be transmitted nonverbally. Crossing the weapons will often be a defensive maneuver. Crossing the legs away from another individual will also show a person's discomfort or a dislike.

Other subtle signals, including the large expansion of the arm, can sometimes help us to seem bigger and more comfortable while maintaining the arms close to the body. When you try to measure your body language a little, be careful about some of the following signals that your legs and arms will transmit to you from the target:

Crossed arms: This will give you a signal that you're closed, safe and defensive. As a manipulator, you need to uncross the arms of the goal to make you feel comfortable.

Standing on hips with your hands: This can be a good sign that the person is ready and controlled. This will sometimes be a sign of aggression.

Clamp the hands so that they're behind the back: This will be a sign that your goal is angry, anxious or boring. You have to look at some of the other signals that come first.

Tap fingers or fidgeting quickly: The other person is frustrated, impatient and even bored.

Crossed legs: This is a good indication that someone feels closed or needs some privacy.

Posture is another thing you should look at. The way we hold our bodies will also be a significant component of body language. Posture refers to how we hold our bodies and to a person's general physical shape. Posture can give a wealth of data on how someone feels and also suggests that a person's features are submissive, open or confident.

For instance, if you sit directly, it can show that an individual is concentrated and is attempting to look after what is going on. Sitting down with the body, on the other side, will show that someone is most of the time indifferent or bored. Looking at your goal will assist you to understand whether you are interested in what you do or say, or if you need to move on to find a different destination.

Whenever you attempt to read some of the languages of your body, attempt and find out some signals that your goal's position is attempting to tell you. Some of them are:

Open posture. Open posture. This includes keeping the body's trunk exposed and open. This sort of

Closed position: this one will require hiding the body's trunk and hitting the legs and arms. This posture will be more indicative of anxiety, discomfort, and depression in the objective.

The eyes clues to revealing true intentions

The visual gateway to the globe around us is our eyes. When

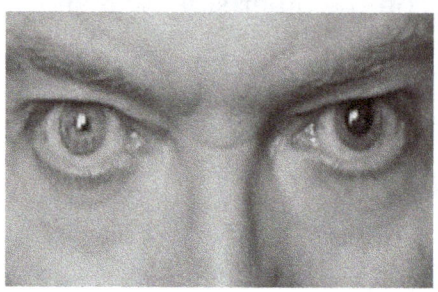 we are born, we scan for data in the familiar face, motion or novelty, color, shade, symmetry and always for aesthetic pleasure.

Our visual cortex, which is big in ratio to the remainder of the brain, is looking for fresh things and fresh experiences. Our eyes demonstrate love and compassion and fear and contempt. Welcome or happy eyes can create our day. But eyes can also let us know that something is wrong, that issues or issues exist. In a crowd of strangers, the eyes can own space or cower. We adorn our eyes so that we can attract and prevent them.

Signs of the shoulders neck and hips

Shoulders

Some identifiers will be explained below. An ear-raised shoulder when an individual answers a question is generally insecurity or doubt. In combination with other behaviors, this indicates well that a person lacks trust in what he says (hesitation in answering, arms drawing closer to the body). When a party raises a single shoulder in negotiations in reaction to a question such as "Is that your best price? It usually indicates that there is space for negotiation. A one-shoulder response indicates that there is no complete commitment to what is said. The slow, deliberate increase of one shoulder combined with a bent head to the same shoulder while making direct contact with the eye represents a private interest. We generally see this in dating circumstances, generally in females who look like someone. When individuals are asked a question and do not understand the response, they lift rapidly and prominently both shoulders.

Neck

Beyond a scratch, neck touch is a good measure of insecurity,

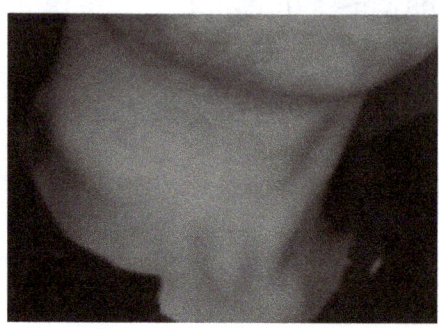

fear, anxiety, concerns or problems. However, we tend to touch our neck slightly if something disturbs us or concerns us. Neck touch is often ignored in all its forms and yet it's one of the most accurate when it comes to exposing something that bothers us. The touch or covering of the "neck dimple" or suprasternal notch (the region of the indented throat under the Adam apple and just above the upper thorn) shows concern, concern, worry, insecurity or anxiety. Men tend to grab or cover this area robustly by their hands while adjusting or grabbing their collar. Women touch this region more often than males, and with the tips of their fingers they tend to do so more lightly. Whether delicately or forcefully, the weakest point of the body means something is at stake. When we feel threatened, our neck developed most probably as a consequence of the innumerable encounters our species experienced numerous acts of predation by the big felines which generally go for the neck. See what everybody is saying for more data.

Hips

Hip swiveling is a way to deal with stress, boredom or

exhaustion in a single location. People could do this, either when their feelings are rallied or afterward, in controversial discussions, as a method of calming down. Under pressure, individuals are rubbed as a pacifier by their hips and legs. It is also used for drying sweaty hands when you feel nervous. You see this gesture as learners prepare for an exam or as people pass customs. Persons under psychological stress can rock back and forth on the hips while sitting. Serious stress such as witnessing a loved one's death will trigger this conduct, which pacifies with its repetitive movement. This conduct could also be seen in individuals with certain mental illnesses such as autism. If we're bored, we might stand and swing our hips, as if we were cradling and sleeping a child.

Mimic body language

Mimicking is a social phenomenon in which people imitate the posture, gestures, and words of another person. Often it is unconscious conduct–we rarely know this when we do–but it's a sign that individuals are in harmony and synchronization with one another. When two persons look at each other, it demonstrates convenience, trust, and relationship between them. Long-term friends and romantic couples are especially attuned. You will often notice couples mirror themselves as they communicate if you ever go to a populous pubic region, such as a park, a mall or a busy road. As social humans, it is part of our basic nature. For instance, in my apartment, I have a balcony over a busy road in Brooklyn.

Chapter 7 Facial Expression and Hand Movements

The universal facial expressions are a set of seven different expressions that people can understand and read, regardless of culture or how much or little they are raised with others. Even those who are born blind will still show these facial expressions without having ever seen them before, leading psychologists to believe that these expressions absolutely are innate in human beings as a whole. These expressions are usually sorted out by the emotion they represent.

Surprise: When someone is exhibiting surprise, they usually raise their eyebrows, with the centers raising higher than the edges, creating a rounded look, and also pushing up skin onto the forehead, creating wrinkles. The eyes are wide, with whites being flashed both above and below the iris. Oftentimes, the mouth is opened loosely and without tension.

Fear: When afraid, people usually raise their eyebrow, but instead of them being rounded, they are instead relatively straight. The individual who is afraid will also show a wrinkled forehead in the center, typically between the eyebrows. They also usually show widened eyes, but the whites of the eye are seen from the top part of the eye and not the bottom. The mouth may be open slightly, with lips parted and pulled back with some tenseness.

Disgust: When someone looks at something in disgust, usually the eyelids are raised up with the brows dropped lower. The nose is usually wrinkled while paired with a raised upper lip. The wrinkling of the nose usually causes lines underneath the eyes, at the top part of the cheek.

Anger: Anger is quite easily recognized at a glance. When someone is angry, their brows are lowered and knitted together, creating wrinkles between the brows running vertically. The eyes stare harshly, with the lids tensed. The lips will be either sealed shut firmly, frowning, or wide open if yelling.

Happiness: When genuinely happy, people usually smile. Their lips pull upward, and they sometimes flash their teeth while smiling. There is usually a discernable line running from the nose to the corners of the lips, and there should be creases around the eyes when genuinely happy.

Sadness: When people feel sad, their eyebrows draw together, with the inner corners raising upwards, creating wrinkles between them. The lips are pulled downward in a frown, and the jaw is raised upwards. Oftentimes the lip is pushed outward in a pout.

Contempt: Contempt is largely characterized by a neutral expression with the corner of the mouth raised on one side and a hard stare.

Eyes

The eyes have several different forms of nonverbal communication—from where they look to how they move plenty can be told about someone's inner thoughts by paying special attention to the eyes.

Eye contact: When people intentionally make eye contact, pay attention to how it is regulated. If the person avoids eye contact, they likely want to end an interaction or avoid an interaction due to insecurity, disinterest, submission, or even deceit. Conversely, making eye contact with others shows interest, and when it is forced and held in a hard manner, it implies dominance and aggression.

Frequency of blinking: People blink at different rates depending on whether they are honest or not. Those who are blinking more than normal are usually under some sort of stress, perhaps due to attempting to figure out how to navigate a difficult situation, or possibly due to trying to come up with a convincing lie to sell to other people. Those who blink less are seen as aggressive or dominant.

Pupil dilation: Though far more difficult to recognize at a glance, especially if the other person has dark eyes, pupil dilation tells a lot about a person. Someone with dilated pupils is either attracted to the person he or she is talking with or lost in some pretty intensive thought.

Direction of gaze: People regularly look at what they are interested in. If you notice someone is repeatedly glancing away from you, whether at an exit or at another person, it is a cue that the other person wants to leave and go interact with whatever keeps drawing his or her gaze. It can also be used to tell which side of the brain is actively working — when people look to the left, they are recalling truthful information while those who are looking to the right are typically using the creative parts of their brains that are responsible for telling lies.

Mouth

People oftentimes may be so focused on censoring the words

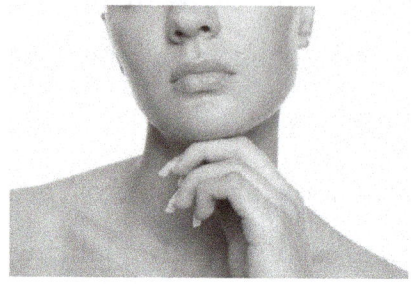

that come out of their mouths that they forget that they must also pay attention to how the mouth moves. People's mouths are awfully telling in terms of how they are moving.

Relaxed lips: When someone is sitting with relaxed lips, they are usually feeling confident and comfortable in their situation.

Parted lips: People part their lips for several reasons. Most commonly, they are attracted to the person they are interacting with, or they are trying to get a word in or to catch the attention of another person.

Baring teeth: This is either good or bad with no in-between — the individual is either smiling, which conveys positive emotions, or snarling, which is conveying anger or aggression.

Twitching lips: Lips can twitch for several reasons ranging from feeling contempt to trying to hide something.

Biting lip or cheek: Oftentimes, people may chew on their lip or cheek when they are feeling nervous. They are attempting to self-soothe through this action. It can also convey deception; however, such as if the person is trying to censor his speech.

Touching mouth with hand: This is another sign that can have several meanings—it could imply that the other person is stressed out and self-soothing, just like when biting the lip or cheek, or it could be a sign of deception or feeling distrustful toward the other party.

Eyebrows

Just like the mouth and eyes, the eyebrows are incredibly
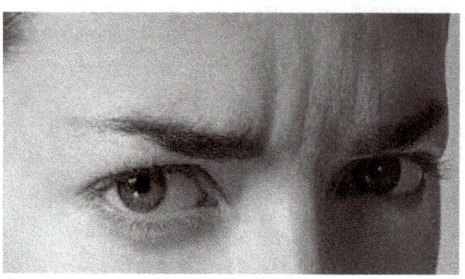
telling about what someone else is thinking. Take a look at these common forms of nonverbal communication involving the eyebrows:

Lowered brows: When someone exhibits lowered brows, he may be showing signs of wanting to hide or retreat, especially if the person is lowering the head. This can also be a sign of deception, in which the individual is attempting to hide.

Raised brows: When someone raises their eyebrows, they signify that they are feeling surprised, or is used to emphasize something that is being said. It may also be used to show attraction to the other person, or sometimes, even submission.

Single brow raised: One brow raised usually comes along with the connotation of disbelief or cynicism.

Knitted brows: This is when the individual pulls the brows together, creating creases in the gap between the brows. It usually shows sadness or confusion.

Middle of brows raised: When the middle of the brows arch upwards, it shows surprise, anxiety, or relief, depending on the context and other parts of the expressions.

Middle of brows lowered: When the middle of the brow is lowered, creating a straight line instead of curving, it usually conveys frustration of some sort.

Body Language

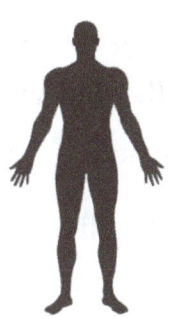

Beyond expressions, people's bodies are actually quite expressive. Just because the hands do not have eyes and a mouth does not mean that you cannot look at the hands of someone else and recognize what they might be feeling.

Head

The head can express so much more than what is plastered on the face. Take a look at some of these ways people communicate without words without the face.

Head tilt: You know what this is — it is the look that a puppy gives you when you say something that it does not understand. When humans tilt their heads, it is for slightly different reasons. Oftentimes, people tilt their heads toward an individual with whom they have rapport, or if they assume that that particular person has authority. When someone tilts their head away, it usually means that the individual is unsure and suspicious of the situation as a whole.

Nod: The nod is the sign of affirmation. It tells the other person that you are listening, even if you are not looking at the speaker at that moment. It identifies that the individual is actively listening to the other party. Pay attention to the speed at which people nod — doing so quickly typically implies that someone is waiting for you to wrap up speaking whereas slower, patient nodding is typically a good thing, implying that the other person feels patient and willing to continue listening.

Position of the chin: The chin can also be quite telling, surprisingly enough. When the chin is raised up, flashing the neck, it shows arrogance or authority. When it is tucked in, however, it implies sadness and insecurity.

Arms

Arms can be used to do a wide variety of different things in  order to convey what an individual is feeling. Take a look at some of these common ways to hold the arms when communicating nonverbally.

Crossed arms: This often conveys defensiveness in some way. It is typically done when the individual wants to protect or guard himself. If the individual has arms crossed with thumbs up, it implies that the individual feels confident in the situation, but still feels the need to be defensive just in case.

Still arms: When the arms are completely still, resting neutrally on either side, or one arm is reached across the body to still the other arm, it implies deception. The individual is physically attempting to control his behavior.

Arms pulled back: When the arms and shoulders are pulled back, the individual is conveying a feeling of defensiveness. With the arms pulled out of reach, the individual is making him less vulnerable to an attack.

Arms raised up: Oftentimes, people raise their arms upward in some sort of exaggeration, regardless of whether it is exaggerating joy, anger, or even confusion. Pay attention to other body language to get a better read on this.

Arms expanded: When the arms are expanded outward, or drawn inward, you can tell the mood. When the arms are expanded outward, they are usually far more relaxed, whereas drawing inward usually conveys stress or tenseness.

Hands

Hands can be quite difficult to track simply because there are so many different positions they can make. Here are the most common nonverbal communications through the hand's body language.

Hands behind back: This implies confidence — the individual is making him entirely vulnerable with hands hidden behind him. It exudes confidence and authority.

Hands-on hips: Typically misconstrued as aggressive but is actually used to show someone is at the ready. You see this pose often with people that must show that they are an authority figure in some way to show assertiveness.

Hands in pockets: This shows that the individual is reluctant or distrusting toward the situation or people around him or her.

Rubbing hands: Rubbing the hands together often shows an eagerness or anticipation for what is about to come.

Fists clenched: When someone's fists are clenched, they come across as firm and stubborn. They show that they will not back down and may also be aggressive.

Chapter 8 How Are They Breathing?

There are different ways you can read someone's body language. It can be read by their leg and arm movements, facial expressions, eye contact, or smiles. Do you realize that how a person breathes has meaning, too?

Emotions and how you breathe are connected. You could read a person's feelings by watching the way they breathe. If emotions change, how they breathe might be affected. See if you can notice breathing patterns in your family, friends, coworkers, or significant other. They may not tell you exactly how they are feeling, and it might depend on certain situations.

Deep breathing might indicate excitement, attraction, anger, fear, or love

Deep breathing is the easiest pattern to notice. If somebody suddenly starts to hold their breath, they might be feeling a little scared. If someone takes a deep breath and then shouts, they could be angry. Excited people are experiencing shock or are surprised might suck in a deep breath. They might also take in a deep breath and hold it for a few seconds. If their eyes start to glow, this might indicate that they are surprised or excited. A person might start to breathe deeply if they feel an attraction toward another person. You may notice someone take a deep breath in, suck in their stomach, and push their chest out to try and impress somebody they are attracted to.

Sighing might signal hopelessness, sadness, or relief

When you sigh, you are letting out a deep, long breath that you can hear. Somebody might sigh if they are feeling relieved after a struggle has passed. They are thankful that their struggle is over. A sign might show sadness or hopelessness like somebody who is waiting for a date to show up. It could also show tiredness and disappointment.

Rapid, heavy breathing might show fear and tiredness

You may have just seen a person rob a place, and they are being chased by the police. You notice they are breathing very rapidly. This is because their lungs need more oxygen since they are exerting a lot of energy. After all, they are running. Their bodies feel tired, and their lungs are trying their best to keep up. We feel the same effects when we feel scared. This will happen when we experience fear; our lungs need more oxygen, so we begin to breathe faster.

Another interesting fact about breath is that smells can influence breath. Any odors that are tied to emotions can change a person's respiration rate. There have been several studies that have shown that the body will respond to bad and good smells by breathing differently. If you were to smell something rotten, you would end up breathing in a shallow and rapid manner. But, if, instead, you smelled baking bread and roses, your breath would be slow and long.

According to Scientific American, the emotions that we have with smells and scents are extremely associative. We started learning about these different smells in the womb, and then during our lives, our brains learn to refine our views of emotional rewards, pleasures, and threats that are contained within a certain odor. If a person breathes deeply, then they feel that something is safe, and it creates a pleasurable emotional state. This means if you notice a person's breathing rate suddenly changes, let your sense of smell catch up first. It could be that they have gotten a whiff of something they either like or dislike.

The interesting thing is that while we can learn how a person feels based on how they are breathing, the way a person breathes can also affect their emotions. In a 2006 study published in Behavior Response & Therapy, they discovered that undergraduates who practiced slow-breathing exercises for 15 minutes had a more positive and balanced emotional response afterward than the group who were faced with 15 minutes of unfocused worrying and attention.

And it doesn't even have to do with just being calm. In a study by the French scientist Pierre Phillipot, he asked some participants to identify the pattern of breath that they connected with certain emotions such as sadness and joy. The results they got were amazing. If the subjects were told to breathe in a particular manner, even if they were unaware of it, they said that they felt the feeling associated emotion, apparently, out of nowhere.

I want to share one more way you can use a person's breath to tell how they feel. This is something that you can't readily do, but it is still interesting.

A new idea that is being studied about emotions and breath is that what you exhale also plays a role in emotional response and that the chemically analyzed exhales were able to figure out how the person felts. In an article from Science News, the chemical makeup of the air within a soccer stadium varies when people begin cheering, and the same is true in movie theaters. They studied 9500 people as they watched 16 different films that ranged from rom-coms to horrors, and then they studied the air composition of the room to see if it changed during certain scenes that were rather emotional in one way or the other.

The crazy thing is that it did. In suspenseful moments, there were more CO_2 and isoprenes in the air, which are chemicals associated with the tensing of muscles. Every type of emotion came with its chemical makeup.

Facial Micro expressions

Learning to decode facial expressions is similar to having superpowers. The face, with all its expressions, which are called micro expressions, could be a window into their soul. Knowing how to read them could help you to understand a lot about how someone is feeling.

Methods of Nonverbal Analysis

For you to perform any nonverbal behavior analysis, you have to use techniques that can help you describe the behavior in a way so it can be trusted. The advantages of scientific analysis are:

To select a person's weaknesses and strengths during normal relations.

To expose lies by using a combination of facial and verbal expressions.

To anticipate a person's behavior.

To identify another person's state of mind and emotions.

Scientific Based

The very first text that was written about emotional expressions was written by a French neurologist, Guillaume Benjamin Amand Duchenne de Boulogne. This text was written in 1862 and demonstrated the method of using electrodes on the facial muscles to establish their relationship between the movements of the facial muscles and the subsequent emotional expression. To honor him, a true, authentic smile can sometimes be called the Duchenne smile.

The Expressions of the Emotions in Man and Animals was written by Charles Darwin in 1872. In this, he says that emotions are just another evolutionary product and are inherited. Body and facial expressions go hand in hand with emotions and look to be the same in people who live in different parts of the world and other animals and primates. Darwin's studies didn't continue after he died because of the hostility within the scientific community toward his theories and him. He was criticized for saying animals have emotions. According to his critics, only humans can feel things. His methods were based on observations rather than science.

This concept of emotional expressions being universal was discovered one more time in the late 1950s. Researchers like Birdwhistell, Izard, Ekman, Ellsworth, and Friesen tried to get Darwin's theory validated. All of them worked together to develop a set of theories, tests, and methods that created the "Facial Expression Program." They believed the origin of emotional expressions and emotional experiences would be a specific number of inherited neurological programs. We know now that there are specific paths for every emotion that causes a facial expression that is associated with that particular emotion. According to the theory of evolution, emotions have adaptive functions that will let a human react through immediate responses to various stimuli for survival.

There are two groups of nonverbal techniques:

Decoding technique: This interprets and will give meaning to movements.

Coding technique: This describes the body and facial movements.

Facial Expression Techniques

ISFE or Interpretative System of Facial Expressions

Jasna Legisa developed this in the NeuroComScience laboratory in 2013. It is a table of what facial movements mean. It is comprised of a set of descriptions and tables that order and integrate facial expressions according to the emotions they are related to. This information was taken from existing literature and previous systems about this subject.

Other than secondary and primary emotional expressions, other facial signs get described as regulators, illustrators, and manipulators. According to Ekman, Izard, and Hjorstjo, emotional expressions get grouped into "big families." All of these "families" include many facial expressions that, even though they mean slightly different things, get united because they receive the same emotional range. Within the "surprise" family, you will have an annoying surprise, face surprise, a real surprise, awe, and many more.

Primary emotional movements get put into three categories:

The first category includes muscular movements that belong to specific emotions.

The second category includes movements that might belong to primary emotions.

The third category includes minor variations to emotions that could be part of many emotional families.

These categorizations make the interpretation and accuracy of the whole analysis.

Mimic Language and Man's Face or the Hjorstjo Method

An anatomy professor at Lund University located in Sweden, Hjorstjo, in 1969, tried to systematically categorize certain facial movements with their meanings into eight emotional families.

MAX or Maximally Discriminative Coding System

This system gives meaning to the facial movements instead of just describing them. Izard developed MAX in 1979. Later in 1983, he worked with Hembree and Dougherty to create an advanced version of MAX that was named AFFEX. The created facial configurations that were based on regular expressions of emotions like shame, disgust, pain, surprise, happiness, interest, fear, sadness, and anger. Basically, for every emotion and expression gets classified.

EMACS or Emotional Facial Action Coding System

Friesen and Ekman worked to describe the expressions of six emotional families: fear, surprise, anger, disgust, sadness, and happiness. Hager has been working at Ekman's laboratory since 1994, studying facial expressions by using an automatic computer to identify their techniques. This database has created the FACSAID or FACS Affect Interpretation Dictionary system.

Hanes

During the same year that the first version of FACS was published, the Hanest Manual was also published. The Hanest Manual was created by Gergerian and Emiane, who are two French scientists. It has the same plan of FACS to describe facial movements.

FACS or Facial Action Coding System

Vincent W. Friesen and Paul Ekman in 1978 introduced FACS or the Facial Action Coding System. In 2002, while working with Hager, they release another version. This one is a descriptive facial coding system, and it doesn't ascribe meaning to facial expressions. It contains detailed descriptions of changes that happen because of facial movements.

CONCLUSION

Congratulations on making it to the end.

Now a day, during hiring interviews, companies hire psychologists to sit on the jury that judges candidates to determine how emotionally intelligent a person is or not. Even tests now take place a day before hiring to gauge your emotional intelligence because it's an essential technical skill to have. And not only during the recruitment process, but also during the promotion committees, each candidate is fully evaluated and their emotional intelligence is ranked. The higher you rise in the hierarchy / chain of command, the more work and people you are responsible for, so excellent leadership skills are increasingly concentrated. As we have found, good leaders have good emotional intelligence. Technical skills are essential, but also control over emotions.

Good luck.

CPSIA information can be obtained
at www.ICGtesting.com
Printed in the USA
BVHW050907070421
604337BV00006B/991